JOSH STEVE

A Stock Market Mystery

Copyright © 2023 by Josh Steve

All rights reserved. No part of this publication may be reproduced, stored or transmitted in any form or by any means, electronic, mechanical, photocopying, recording, scanning, or otherwise without written permission from the publisher. It is illegal to copy this book, post it to a website, or distribute it by any other means without permission.

This novel is entirely a work of fiction. The names, characters and incidents portrayed in it are the work of the author's imagination. Any resemblance to actual persons, living or dead, events or localities is entirely coincidental.

Josh Steve asserts the moral right to be identified as the author of this work.

First edition

This book was professionally typeset on Reedsy. Find out more at reedsy.com

Contents

The Disappearing Millions	1
The Red Flag Emerges	4
The Wall Street Whispers	8
The Enigmatic Trader	12
Intricate Web of Deception	16
The Dangerous Alliance	20
The Prague Connection	24
The Trading Floor's Secret	27
The Tipping Point	32
The Midnight Showdown	35
The Unmasking	39
The Final Confrontation	42

The Disappearing Millions

The New York Stock Exchange, a bustling hive of financial activity, stood tall against the vibrant cityscape. Investors and traders rushed through the colossal bronze doors, ready to make or lose fortunes in the blink of an eye. Among them, Michael Stratton, a seasoned stock market analyst with graying temples, strode purposefully toward the iconic Wall Street Bull sculpture.

It was an ordinary Tuesday morning, but today would mark the beginning of an extraordinary mystery. Michael's polished black shoes clicked against the cobblestone streets as he made his way to the brokerage firm, Wallington & Co., his employer of over a decade. As he entered the building, the aroma of freshly brewed coffee mixed with the low hum of financial jargon filled the air.

"Morning, Michael," greeted Sarah, the receptionist. Her smile was bright but fleeting, as she was busy fielding calls and greeting clients.

"Morning, Sarah," Michael replied with a nod, his eyes scanning the bustling trading floor as he moved through the maze of desks and computer terminals. The energy here was palpable, fueled by ambition and the promise of wealth.

Michael's office, tucked away in a corner, was adorned with certificates, accolades, and a skyline view that seemed to promise limitless possibilities.

His computer screen displayed a bewildering array of stock tickers and charts, a world he navigated with the ease of a seasoned sailor.

He settled into his leather chair, sipping the coffee he'd picked up from the lobby. He was preparing for a routine morning meeting with his team when a message flashed on his screen. It was an alert that caught his attention:

"Abnormal Activity Detected: WGC Holdings."

WGC Holdings was a high-profile hedge fund with billions under management. Known for its remarkable consistency in returns, it was considered the golden goose of Wall Street. Michael's fingers danced across the keyboard as he dove into the analysis.

Minutes felt like hours as he scrutinized the data. His brow furrowed, and he couldn't believe what he was seeing. It was as if a massive chunk of WGC's assets had vanished overnight. Billions had been wiped out, disappearing into thin air like a magician's illusion.

"Sarah!" Michael called urgently, his heart pounding in his chest.

Sarah rushed into his office, concern etched across her face. "What's wrong?"

"Pull up everything you can find on WGC Holdings," Michael demanded. "I need to know what's going on."

Sarah nodded, her fingers flying over her keyboard. Within moments, a flurry of news articles and stock analysis reports filled the screen. The headlines were shocking:

"Unprecedented Losses at WGC: Panic Grips Investors."

"SEC Launches Investigation into WGC Holdings."

As Michael read through the articles, a deep sense of unease settled over him. This wasn't just a market correction; this was a financial catastrophe in the making. He couldn't fathom how such a reputable hedge fund could hemorrhage money at this rate.

"Michael, there's something you need to see," Sarah said, her voice trembling. She opened a news video, and Michael watched in shock as the CEO of WGC Holdings, Robert Wendell, held a press conference. Wendell, usually poised and confident, appeared disheveled and anxious.

"We are investigating the situation," Wendell stammered. "But rest assured, we will recover the missing assets and restore confidence in our fund."

Michael leaned back in his chair, his mind racing. Something was profoundly wrong here, and it sent shivers down his spine. He had seen market crashes, bubbles burst, and scandals unfold, but this was different. It felt like the first ominous note of a sinister symphony, and he was determined to unravel the mystery.

As Michael continued to dig into the data, he couldn't shake the feeling that he was standing at the precipice of a financial catastrophe that could rock Wall Street to its core. Rogue traders and red flags were emerging from the shadows, and Michael Stratton was about to embark on a journey that would test his skills, his instincts, and his very understanding of the stock market. The disappearing millions were just the beginning of a mystery that would change his life forever.

The Red Flag Emerges

The following morning dawned with a heavy mist cloaking the New York skyline. Michael Stratton's restless night had been filled with thoughts of the disappearing billions and the enigma that was WGC Holdings. As he sipped his coffee in the predawn darkness of his office, he knew that uncovering the truth behind this financial debacle would require more than just his analytical skills—it would demand every ounce of his determination.

The soft chime of his phone disrupted his contemplation. It was a call from his team. He pressed the answer button and was met with the concerned voices of Emily and David, his two most trusted colleagues.

"Michael, have you seen the news?" Emily's voice quivered with a mix of shock and anxiety.

"Of course," Michael replied, "It's hard to miss. I've been up all night trying to make sense of it."

David chimed in, "We've pulled all the data we could find on WGC Holdings. It's not just the losses; it's how they happened. It doesn't make any sense."

Michael nodded, even though his colleagues couldn't see him through the phone. "I agree. Something's not right here. We need to dig deeper."

THE RED FLAG EMERGES

The team assembled in Michael's office, and they spent hours pouring over charts, financial statements, and trading records. What they discovered was deeply troubling. The losses incurred by WGC Holdings had occurred in an unusually short span of time, and the trades responsible for the hemorrhage were both erratic and untraceable.

Emily pointed to a particular set of transactions on her screen. "Look at this, Michael. Massive sell orders executed at odd hours when the markets were less liquid. It's as if they were trying to hide the trades."

Michael furrowed his brow. "You're right, Emily. These patterns suggest deliberate manipulation of the market. But why? And by whom?"

David interjected, "There's more. We've been tracking the traders behind these unusual transactions. We couldn't identify most of them, but one name keeps popping up—Viktor Petrov."

Viktor Petrov was an elusive figure rumored to operate in the shadows of the financial world. Known for his uncanny ability to profit from market turbulence, he was whispered about in hushed tones by traders who believed he held dark secrets.

Michael leaned forward, studying Viktor Petrov's trading history. "We need to find out everything we can about this guy. And we should notify the SEC about our findings. If Petrov is involved, it could be a clear case of market manipulation."

Emily nodded in agreement. "I'll draft a report and send it to the SEC right away."

As the day wore on, the tension in Michael's office grew palpable. The more they unraveled the mystery, the more questions surfaced. Why would Petrov target WGC Holdings? Did he have inside information? Was he working alone, or was there a larger conspiracy at play?

Just as Michael was about to call it a day, Sarah, the receptionist, buzzed in, her voice trembling over the intercom. "Michael, there's someone here to see you. He says it's urgent."

Michael exchanged puzzled glances with his team. He wasn't expecting any visitors. "Send him in," he said cautiously.

The door to his office swung open, revealing a tall, well-dressed man in his early forties. His sharp eyes surveyed the room, and he carried an air of confidence that bordered on arrogance.

"Michael Stratton?" the man inquired, extending his hand.

Michael nodded, though he couldn't hide his skepticism. "That's me. What can I do for you?"

The man introduced himself as Thomas Everett, a private investigator with a reputation for solving complex financial mysteries. He explained that he had been following the WGC Holdings case closely and believed he had critical information to share.

"Intriguing," Michael said, gesturing for Thomas to take a seat. "Please, tell us what you know."

Thomas leaned forward, his voice hushed. "I've been tracking Viktor Petrov for some time now. He's not just a rogue trader; he's a pawn in a much larger game. And I believe I know who's pulling the strings."

The room fell silent as Thomas Everett began to reveal a web of intrigue that stretched far beyond their initial suspicions. He spoke of powerful figures in the financial world, hidden agendas, and a conspiracy that threatened to plunge not only WGC Holdings but the entire stock market into chaos.

Michael, Emily, and David exchanged glances, realizing that they were on the cusp of a revelation that could change the course of their investigation. As Thomas Everett continued to unravel the tangled threads of this intricate mystery, the stakes grew higher, and the shadows that cloaked the truth deepened. They were about to embark on a perilous journey where every step could lead them closer to uncovering the sinister forces at play, or into the abyss of financial ruin. The red flags were multiplying, and the game had only just begun.

The Wall Street Whispers

The sun dipped below the horizon, casting long shadows across the canyons of Wall Street. Inside the confines of Wallington & Co., Michael Stratton, Emily, David, and Thomas Everett sat huddled around Michael's desk, their faces etched with a mixture of anticipation and trepidation. The revelations from Thomas had sent shockwaves through their investigation, and the path ahead was shrouded in uncertainty.

"Are you telling us that there's a powerful group orchestrating this whole scheme?" Michael asked, his voice low and urgent.

Thomas nodded gravely. "Yes, and it goes by the name 'The Syndicate.' They're a shadowy organization that manipulates financial markets for their own gain. Viktor Petrov is just one of their pawns."

Emily's eyes widened. "But why WGC Holdings? What's their connection to The Syndicate?"

Thomas leaned back in his chair, taking a moment to choose his words carefully. "The Syndicate is always on the lookout for opportunities to destabilize markets and profit from the chaos. WGC Holdings was seen as a fortress—a symbol of financial stability. If they could break it, they could send shockwaves through the entire financial world."

David chimed in, "So, Petrov's erratic trades were meant to destabilize WGC?"

"Exactly," Thomas confirmed. "But we need to dig deeper to understand how Petrov is connected to The Syndicate and who else might be involved."

As they brainstormed their next steps, Sarah, the receptionist, buzzed in again, her voice quivering with urgency. "Michael, you have a visitor. He insists on seeing you."

Michael exchanged a glance with his team, then nodded. "Send him in."

The door swung open, and a man in his late fifties with salt-and-pepper hair entered the room. His suit was impeccably tailored, and he exuded an air of authority. He introduced himself as Daniel Thornton, a senior executive at WGC Holdings.

"I heard about your investigation," he began without preamble, his eyes darting around the room as if he expected eavesdroppers. "I believe we have mutual interests."

Michael raised an eyebrow. "Mutual interests?"

Daniel leaned in, lowering his voice to a conspiratorial whisper. "I have reason to believe that there are individuals within our organization who are working with Petrov and, by extension, The Syndicate. I want to help you uncover the truth and put an end to this before it brings down our entire company."

The room fell into a heavy silence as Michael, Emily, David, and Thomas exchanged wary glances. Trusting a high-ranking executive from the very organization they were investigating was a risky proposition.

"Why should we trust you?" Emily finally asked, her voice laced with skepticism.

Daniel sighed, running a hand through his hair. "Because I've seen the evidence, and I'm convinced that Petrov and The Syndicate are not just a threat to WGC Holdings, but to the entire financial system. If we don't stop them, the fallout will be catastrophic."

After a tense discussion, the team decided to cautiously accept Daniel's offer of assistance. He provided them with confidential documents, internal emails, and access to information that had previously been hidden from the public eye. It was a treasure trove of leads and potential clues.

Over the next several days, Michael and his team worked tirelessly to analyze the new information. They uncovered a trail of cryptic messages exchanged between Petrov and certain WGC Holdings executives. It was clear that these insiders were assisting Petrov in executing his trades and manipulating the market.

As the pieces of the puzzle began to come together, Emily exclaimed, "This is it! We have the proof we need to expose the collusion between Petrov and WGC Holdings executives."

Michael nodded, his eyes gleaming with determination. "We'll take this evidence to the SEC. It's time to shine a light on The Syndicate and all those involved."

With their case growing stronger by the day, the team prepared to take their findings to the authorities. But as they delved deeper into the investigation, they couldn't shake the feeling that they were just scratching the surface of a much larger and more insidious conspiracy. The Wall Street whispers had grown into a cacophony of deceit, and the shadows that concealed the truth were beginning to fray. The Syndicate was a formidable adversary, and Michael Stratton and his team were about to engage in a high-stakes game of financial espionage, where the stakes were not just money but the very integrity of the market itself.

The Enigmatic Trader

In the heart of New York City, the skyline glittered with a thousand lights as night descended upon Wall Street. Inside the dimly lit office of Wallington & Co., Michael Stratton sat hunched over his computer, meticulously going through the evidence they had gathered. The weight of the investigation bore down on him, a constant reminder of the financial storm that loomed.

Emily and David were engrossed in their own work, tracing the intricate web of connections between Viktor Petrov, The Syndicate, and the corrupt WGC Holdings executives. But one name stood out like a beacon in the darkness—Alaric Kane.

"Guys, I think I've found something," David announced, his eyes locked on his computer screen.

Michael swiveled his chair to face David. "What is it?"

David pointed to a series of encrypted messages. "These messages mention someone named Alaric Kane. Petrov seems to rely on him for something crucial, but we can't decipher what it is."

Emily chimed in, her brow furrowed in concentration. "Alaric Kane... I've heard that name before. He's known in the underground trading circles as

'The Enigmatic Trader.' No one knows who he really is, and he's notorious for staying off the grid."

Thomas Everett, who had been quietly observing, leaned forward. "If we can find Alaric Kane, we might uncover the key to Petrov's operations and The Syndicate's plan."

The team set to work, tracing every lead and rumor about the mysterious Alaric Kane. Late into the night, they finally stumbled upon a thread—a cryptic message board frequented by rogue traders, where Alaric Kane's name occasionally surfaced.

Emily monitored the message board, posing as an interested trader. It was a treacherous world of anonymity, where secrets were traded as currency. She engaged with the community, subtly probing for information about Kane.

Days turned into weeks as Emily established herself as a regular on the message board. She shared fictitious trading stories, slowly gaining the trust of some of the more vocal members. But Alaric Kane remained elusive, like a specter hiding in the shadows.

One evening, as the team gathered in Michael's office, Emily burst in with excitement. "I think I've made a breakthrough! One of the users dropped a hint about Alaric Kane's possible whereabouts. It's a remote trading outpost in the Swiss Alps."

Michael's eyes lit up. "Switzerland? That's a long way from Wall Street. But if Kane is there, it's worth investigating. We need to find out what he knows."

The team quickly made arrangements to travel to Switzerland under the guise of a business trip. As they boarded the plane, the gravity of their mission weighed on them. Alaric Kane was their best lead yet, and the fate of WGC Holdings and the entire stock market rested on uncovering his secrets.

The Swiss Alps rose majestically on the horizon as their plane touched down in Zurich. They made their way to a picturesque alpine village named Engadin, nestled among snow-capped peaks. The trading outpost they sought was tucked away in this remote location, far from prying eyes.

Their journey to the outpost was an arduous one, involving treacherous mountain roads and a harrowing cable car ride. As they arrived at their destination, a small cabin perched on the edge of a cliff, the isolation of the place struck them. It was the perfect location for someone like Alaric Kane to conduct clandestine operations.

Inside the cabin, they found an array of computer terminals and trading equipment. It was clear that this was no ordinary outpost. They began to comb through the data, hoping to find clues that would lead them to Alaric Kane.

As they sifted through the digital trail, Michael noticed a locked drawer in one of the desks. With a feeling of trepidation, he picked the lock and found a cache of documents. One of them contained a list of transactions between Viktor Petrov and Alaric Kane, coded in a way that only the two of them could decipher.

"They were in cahoots," Michael muttered, his mind racing. "These transactions hold the key to Petrov's operations."

Emily, who had been examining another document, gasped. "Look at this, guys. Financial records for a Swiss bank account—Alaric Kane's account. It's got to be a substantial sum. If we can trace the source of these funds, we might finally unmask him."

The discovery set off a frenzy of activity as the team pored over the financial records, attempting to follow the money trail. The transactions were complex, involving multiple accounts and shell companies. It was a labyrinthine puzzle that would require time, patience, and unwavering determination to solve.

As night fell over the Swiss Alps, Michael and his team knew that they were closer than ever to unraveling the mystery. Alaric Kane was no longer just an enigmatic name; he was a tangible presence, and they were on his trail. But as they delved deeper into the intricacies of Kane's financial empire, they also realized that they were treading on dangerous ground. The Enigmatic Trader was not a foe to be underestimated, and the secrets he guarded could either save or shatter the world of finance. In this high-stakes game, they had come too far to turn back now.

Intricate Web of Deception

The Swiss Alps stood silent and majestic, their peaks glistening in the early morning sunlight. In the remote cabin in Engadin, Michael Stratton and his team had spent restless nights poring over financial records, attempting to untangle the complex web of transactions linked to Alaric Kane. The Enigmatic Trader's secrets were buried deep within layers of deception, and the team was determined to unearth them.

Emily, David, and Thomas were huddled around the cabin's wooden table, their laptops open and charts strewn about. Michael stood by the window, his gaze fixed on the breathtaking vista outside. The team had been working tirelessly, but the mountain air and the solitude of their surroundings only added to the sense of isolation and urgency.

"We've traced some of the funds," Emily said, her voice tinged with exhaustion. "But it's like chasing a ghost. Every time we think we're getting close, the trail goes cold."

David nodded in agreement. "And the shell companies involved in these transactions are incredibly sophisticated. It's as if they were designed to be untraceable."

Michael turned away from the window, his expression resolute. "We can't afford to give up. Alaric Kane is the linchpin of this operation, and we need to find him. The fate of WGC Holdings and the stability of the stock market hang in the balance."

Thomas Everett, who had been observing the team's progress, chimed in with a thoughtful suggestion. "Perhaps we're approaching this from the wrong angle. Instead of trying to follow the money, we should focus on Petrov. He's the link between Kane and The Syndicate. If we can corner him, he might lead us straight to Kane."

The suggestion resonated with the team. They knew that Viktor Petrov was a rogue trader on the run, and their investigation had uncovered clues suggesting he might be in Eastern Europe. With renewed determination, they redirected their efforts toward tracking down Petrov.

Their search led them to a gritty underworld of shady contacts and black-market connections. They followed a trail of rumors and whispers that took them from Prague to Budapest and finally to a dimly lit underground club in Bucharest, Romania.

As they stepped into the club, the thumping bass and dimly lit corners painted a picture of a world far removed from the polished halls of Wall Street. The air was thick with tension, and the clientele ranged from shadowy figures in tailored suits to tattooed rebels with a penchant for danger.

Thomas, who had cultivated contacts in the region over the years, led the way. He approached a contact at the bar—a man with a scar running down his cheek who went by the name Andrei.

"Andrei," Thomas began in hushed tones, "we're looking for someone—Viktor Petrov. Word is he's been seen around here."

Andrei studied Thomas for a moment, then nodded slowly. "Petrov's been here, all right. He's been playing a dangerous game with some powerful people. But you didn't hear it from me."

With Andrei as their reluctant guide, they navigated a labyrinthine maze of backstreets and hidden passages, descending deeper into the underbelly of Bucharest. Finally, they arrived at a nondescript building that bore no markings of its significance.

Andrei turned to them, his eyes filled with caution. "This is where you'll find Petrov. But be careful—there are eyes everywhere."

The team entered the building, their senses on high alert. The corridor led to a dimly lit room, where Viktor Petrov sat alone at a table, his face obscured by shadows. His sharp eyes, however, locked onto the intruders, and a sense of foreboding filled the room.

Michael cleared his throat, his voice unwavering. "Viktor Petrov, we know about your involvement with The Syndicate and Alaric Kane. We're here for answers."

Petrov's lips curled into a sardonic smile, revealing a glint of defiance. "You're in over your heads, Stratton. You have no idea what you're dealing with."

But Michael was undeterred. "We have evidence that can bring down The Syndicate, and we're willing to share it with the authorities. You can choose to cooperate or face the consequences."

Petrov's laughter echoed through the room, a chilling sound that sent shivers down their spines. "You think you can stop The Syndicate? You're just pawns in a much larger game."

Before Michael could respond, the room plunged into darkness, the only illumination coming from the soft glow of Petrov's laptop. The rogue trader's fingers danced across the keyboard, and a series of cryptic messages appeared on the screen.

"I've sent a signal to The Syndicate," Petrov taunted. "They know you're here, and they won't let you leave."

Panic surged through the team as they heard the approaching footsteps of ominous figures in the corridor outside. They were trapped, deep within the heart of a dangerous game, and Petrov had just raised the stakes. The intricate web of deception was tightening around them, and escape seemed impossible. The Enigmatic Trader's secrets remained tantalizingly out of reach, and they were about to face the full wrath of The Syndicate. In the shadows of that dimly lit room, their battle for the truth had taken a perilous turn.

The Dangerous Alliance

In the dimly lit room, the tension hung heavy as Viktor Petrov's taunting laughter echoed off the walls. Michael Stratton and his team were trapped, and the ominous footsteps drawing nearer in the corridor outside signaled the imminent arrival of danger.

Petrov's laptop screen flickered with a sinister green glow as cryptic messages continued to appear, signaling his communication with The Syndicate. Emily's heart pounded as she scanned the messages, trying to decipher any clues about their situation.

"They're coming," Petrov hissed, a mixture of fear and anticipation in his eyes. "You've sealed your fate by chasing this down."

Michael clenched his fists, his determination unwavering. "We're not here to play games, Petrov. We need answers about The Syndicate and Alaric Kane. Tell us what you know, and maybe, just maybe, we can help you."

Petrov's gaze darted between the team members, and for a moment, it seemed as though he might relent. But then the room's door swung open, and a group of burly figures in dark suits flooded in. Their faces concealed by masks, they exuded an aura of menace.

Without a word, they surrounded Petrov, who seemed to know them well. One of the figures, the apparent leader, stepped forward and spoke in a voice that sent shivers down the team's spines.

"Viktor Petrov, you've been a thorn in our side for far too long. It's time to settle accounts."

The leader raised a small device and pressed a button. A sudden burst of blinding light filled the room, disorienting everyone inside. Michael's team shielded their eyes, but when the glare faded, they found themselves alone in the room, with Petrov and The Syndicate figures gone.

Panic gripped them as they realized that they were now truly on their own in the heart of Bucharest's dark underbelly. They hurriedly scanned the room for any clues Petrov might have left behind, but it appeared that he had wiped his laptop clean of any evidence.

"We have to get out of here," David urged, his voice trembling with urgency.

The team filed out of the room cautiously, moving through the labyrinthine corridors of the building. But the further they ventured into the maze-like structure, the more apparent it became that they were being pursued.

Footsteps echoed through the narrow passages behind them, and they quickened their pace, their hearts pounding. It was a harrowing game of cat and mouse, and their every step felt like a race against time.

As they reached a junction, a sudden decision had to be made. Left or right? They had no way of knowing which path would lead them to safety, and the relentless pursuit was closing in.

With little choice, they veered left, hoping it would take them out of the building. But the corridor seemed endless, and there was no sign of an exit.

Anxiety gnawed at them as they tried to keep their bearings.

Finally, they stumbled upon a door that led to a dark alleyway. The cold night air hit them like a blast of clarity, and they breathed a sigh of relief. The alleyway was narrow, with tall buildings looming on either side, but at least it offered a chance at escape.

Just as they were about to make a run for it, a figure emerged from the shadows, blocking their path. It was Andrei, the contact who had led them to Petrov.

"I can help you," Andrei whispered urgently, a hint of desperation in his eyes. "Petrov and The Syndicate are dangerous. I want out."

Michael exchanged wary glances with his team, but they had no other options. They had to trust him.

"What do you know?" Michael asked, his voice low.

Andrei quickly explained that he had been coerced into working for The Syndicate, forced to act as a liaison in their operations. He had seen Petrov's communications with Kane and knew that Petrov had a contact in Prague—an insider within WGC Holdings—who had been feeding him information.

"We have to go to Prague," Andrei said. "That's where you'll find the link to Alaric Kane."

With Andrei as their guide, they managed to slip through the alleys and streets of Bucharest, making their way to the city's main train station. There, they boarded a night train bound for Prague, their minds racing with the knowledge that they were getting closer to unmasking Alaric Kane and exposing The Syndicate's dangerous alliance.

As the train rumbled through the dark European countryside, Michael and his team couldn't help but reflect on the perilous journey they were on. The Syndicate was a formidable adversary, and the dangers they faced were increasing with each step. But they were driven by a relentless pursuit of the truth and a determination to bring those responsible to justice.

Intrigue and danger lay ahead in the cobblestone streets of Prague, where a mysterious insider held the key to Alaric Kane's secrets. The intricate web of deception was far from unraveled, and the team's alliance with Andrei was a fragile thread in their pursuit of justice. As the night train carried them closer to their destination, they knew that their battle against The Syndicate was far from over, and the stakes were higher than ever.

The Prague Connection

The night train from Bucharest pulled into Prague's bustling central station with a sigh of hydraulic brakes and the clatter of wheels against the platform. It was early morning, and the sun was just beginning to cast its golden rays over the historic city. As Michael Stratton and his team disembarked, they couldn't help but feel a sense of trepidation mixed with determination. Prague held the next piece of the puzzle in their relentless pursuit of The Syndicate and Alaric Kane.

Andrei, their reluctant ally from Bucharest, led the way through the labyrinthine streets of Prague's Old Town. Cobblestone alleys wound between centuries-old buildings, and the air was thick with the echoes of history. The city had an aura of mystique that seemed to mirror the enigma of Alaric Kane.

Their destination was a discreet café nestled within a hidden courtyard. It was the kind of place that whispered secrets, and it was here that Andrei believed they would find the contact from WGC Holdings—an insider who had been colluding with Viktor Petrov.

They entered the café and took a seat at a corner table, scanning the room for any sign of their contact. The café was quiet, save for the low murmur of conversation and the soft jazz playing in the background. Waiters moved gracefully between tables, delivering steaming cups of espresso and flaky pastries.

Minutes stretched into hours as they waited, the tension in the air thickening. Finally, just as they were beginning to lose hope, a man in a dark suit and fedora entered the café. He glanced around, his eyes darting from face to face until they settled on Michael's team.

With a nod, Andrei signaled to the man, who approached their table with an air of caution. He introduced himself as Milan Novak, an employee of WGC Holdings, and the gravity of the situation was etched into the lines on his face.

"You're taking an enormous risk by meeting with us," Michael said, his voice low. "But we need answers about your involvement with Viktor Petrov and Alaric Kane."

Milan sighed, his gaze filled with regret. "I never wanted to be a part of this. They threatened my family, and I had no choice. But I can tell you everything I know."

As Milan began to divulge the details of his involvement, it became clear that he had been feeding Petrov critical information about WGC Holdings' trades and investment strategies. It was a dangerous game he had been forced to play, and he knew that his actions had contributed to the financial instability that now threatened the global markets.

Emily leaned forward, her voice compassionate. "We understand your predicament, Milan. But we need to know how Petrov and Kane are connected. How can we find Alaric Kane?"

Milan's expression darkened. "Alaric Kane is the linchpin. Petrov only knew him through coded messages and never met him in person. But I've heard whispers about a place—a clandestine trading floor where Kane conducts his operations. It's hidden deep within the heart of Prague."

The team exchanged glances. The location of Alaric Kane's trading floor was the breakthrough they had been hoping for. They knew that getting there would be fraught with danger, but they had come too far to turn back now.

Milan continued, "To access Kane's trading floor, you'll need an invitation. Only a select few are granted access, and I can't guarantee anything."

Michael nodded. "We'll take that chance. Tell us how to get there."

Milan provided them with a set of cryptic instructions and a coded message that would serve as their invitation. The trading floor was known to be heavily guarded, and secrecy was paramount.

With the information in hand, the team left the café, their minds racing with the knowledge that they were one step closer to confronting Alaric Kane. But the path ahead was shrouded in uncertainty, and danger lurked around every corner.

As they made their way through Prague's historic streets, the city's ancient buildings seemed to whisper their secrets. The intricate web of deception was closing in, and the stakes were higher than ever. The elusive Alaric Kane was no longer just a name on a screen; he was a tangible presence, and the team was determined to unmask him, no matter the cost.

Their journey through Prague's winding alleys led them to a hidden passage beneath the Charles Bridge, where they would embark on the next leg of their perilous quest. The unknown awaited them, and the dangerous alliance between Petrov, Kane, and The Syndicate was about to face its most formidable adversary—the relentless pursuit of justice.

The Trading Floor's Secret

Beneath the centuries-old arches of the Charles Bridge in Prague, Michael Stratton's team found themselves in a hidden passage that wound its way deep beneath the city's historic streets. The air was damp, and the sound of rushing water from the Vltava River above echoed through the ancient stone walls. They knew that this was the path to the clandestine trading floor where Alaric Kane conducted his operations—a place shrouded in secrecy and guarded by The Syndicate.

The instructions provided by Milan Novak had been cryptic, but they followed them meticulously, taking them through a maze of tunnels and chambers that seemed to have been forgotten by time. The further they ventured into the labyrinth, the more apparent it became that this place held an eerie, almost supernatural quality.

Finally, they reached an unassuming door, barely visible in the dimly lit passage. Michael hesitated for a moment, his hand resting on the doorknob. He knew that what lay beyond could be the key to exposing The Syndicate's dangerous alliance with Alaric Kane.

With a determined twist of the knob, the door creaked open to reveal a world that was unlike anything they had imagined. It was a vast underground chamber, its walls lined with towering screens displaying complex financial data, charts, and graphs. Rows of traders sat at sleek terminals, their fingers dancing across keyboards as they executed trades with precision.

The atmosphere in the chamber was electric, a stark contrast to the ancient passageways they had traversed to reach it. Traders in sharp suits and headsets moved with a sense of purpose, their eyes glued to the screens as they manipulated the markets with calculated moves. It was a high-stakes game unfolding in the shadows.

Michael and his team stood at the entrance, their presence initially unnoticed amidst the controlled chaos of the trading floor. But as they ventured further into the chamber, it didn't take long for the traders to recognize that they were outsiders.

The room fell silent as the traders turned their attention to the intruders. A hushed murmur of conversation rippled through the chamber, and Michael could feel the weight of scrutiny from every corner.

"We need to find Alaric Kane," Michael announced, his voice projecting authority. "We have an invitation."

He held up the coded message provided by Milan Novak, and it seemed to catch the attention of a trader who appeared to be in charge. The man, tall and impeccably dressed, approached with a sense of authority that matched his surroundings.

"I am Anton Kovac," he said, his voice carrying a note of curiosity. "You claim to have an invitation to this trading floor. What is your business here?"

Michael explained their mission—to uncover the truth behind Alaric Kane's operations and expose The Syndicate's dangerous alliance with Petrov. Kovac listened intently, his sharp eyes assessing the team.

Finally, he nodded. "Very well. You may follow me, but you must understand that access to Alaric Kane is highly restricted. We do not take kindly to intruders."

The team followed Kovac through a labyrinth of terminals and traders, their footsteps echoing on the polished floor. As they ventured deeper into the chamber, they couldn't help but feel a sense of unease. The traders in the room seemed to operate with a level of precision that bordered on the uncanny, and the atmosphere was charged with an almost palpable tension.

At last, they reached a section of the chamber that was cordoned off from the rest—a secluded area where Alaric Kane's terminal sat. It was a sleek, state-of-the-art setup, surrounded by a glass barrier that seemed to emphasize Kane's isolation.

Kovac turned to them. "This is as close as you will get to Alaric Kane. You may present your invitation, but be cautious in your interactions with him. He is not one to be trifled with."

With a nod of gratitude, Michael approached the glass barrier, presenting the coded message to Kane's security personnel. Moments later, the glass partition slid open, and they found themselves face to face with the elusive Alaric Kane.

He was a man of mystery, his features hidden behind dark glasses and a meticulously groomed beard. His eyes, however, were sharp and penetrating, as if they could see straight through to their souls.

"I understand you have questions," Kane began, his voice soft and composed. "Ask them."

Michael took a deep breath, acutely aware of the gravity of the moment. "We need to know about your connection to Viktor Petrov and The Syndicate.

We've been tracking the trail of destruction left by your operations, and it's time for answers."

Kane's lips curved into a cryptic smile. "You're more tenacious than I expected. Very well, I'll tell you what you want to know."

As Kane began to speak, his revelations sent shockwaves through Michael and his team. He explained that he had been the mastermind behind The Syndicate's financial schemes, using Petrov and other rogue traders as pawns in a much larger game. The ultimate goal was to amass power and influence over the global financial system, with The Syndicate pulling the strings from the shadows.

But as Kane continued, he revealed a startling truth—that The Syndicate had even deeper connections, reaching into the highest echelons of political and corporate power. It was a dangerous alliance that had allowed them to operate with impunity.

"The Syndicate is not just a group of rogue traders," Kane said, his voice tinged with a hint of remorse. "It is a network of powerbrokers who will stop at nothing to protect their interests. You cannot defeat them."

The weight of Kane's words hung heavy in the air. The team had uncovered a dangerous alliance that reached far beyond their initial suspicions. The Syndicate's web of deception extended into the highest levels of influence, and the truth they sought was a double-edged sword that threatened to expose the very foundations of the financial world.

As they left the clandestine trading floor, Michael and his team couldn't help but reflect on the magnitude of the challenge they faced. The Syndicate was a formidable adversary, and their alliance with Alaric Kane had revealed a depth of corruption that was staggering. The intricate web of deception was far from unraveled, and the journey for justice had taken an unexpected turn—one that would lead them into the heart of a battle against the most powerful forces in the world.

The Tipping Point

The night had descended over Prague, casting long shadows on the city's ancient cobblestone streets. Michael Stratton and his team had left the underground trading floor behind, their minds abuzz with the revelations from their encounter with Alaric Kane. The Syndicate's dangerous alliance extended far beyond what they had initially imagined, and the enormity of their task weighed heavily on their shoulders.

Back at their makeshift base in Prague's historic district, they gathered around a dimly lit table, illuminated only by the glow of their laptops. Milan Novak, the WGC Holdings employee who had been coerced into assisting Petrov, sat with them, his face etched with a mixture of guilt and determination.

"We have to expose The Syndicate's corruption," Michael declared, his voice filled with resolve. "Kane admitted that they have powerful allies within governments and corporations. If we can bring their operations to light, it might be enough to dismantle their network."

Milan nodded, his expression grim. "I'll do whatever it takes to help you. They used my family as leverage, and I can't live with what I've done."

As the team delved into their investigation, they realized that uncovering the depth of The Syndicate's influence would be an uphill battle. The network operated with ruthless efficiency, leaving few traces that could be traced back to them. But they had one advantage—Kane's admission that they had a contact within WGC Holdings, someone who had been providing critical information.

Emily took charge of this part of the investigation, poring over Milan's notes and emails for any leads. Days turned into weeks as she meticulously traced the flow of information, attempting to identify the mole within the company.

One evening, as she sifted through a trove of emails, she stumbled upon a thread that sent a shiver down her spine. It was a series of messages between Milan and a mysterious contact within the company, identified only as "X."

"Milan," Emily said, her voice trembling with urgency, "I think I've found our mole. It's someone high up in WGC Holdings, and they're using the codename 'X.'"

The team gathered around her, their eyes fixed on the screen. The messages revealed a complex web of communication, with "X" providing insider information about WGC Holdings' trades and investment strategies to Milan, who then relayed the information to Petrov.

David leaned in, his brow furrowed in concentration. "We need to expose 'X' and bring them to justice. They could be the key to unraveling The Syndicate's operations."

Michael nodded in agreement. "But we have to be cautious. If 'X' is as deeply embedded within the company as it seems, they'll have powerful allies. Exposing them could be dangerous."

With their new lead, the team began to dig deeper into "X's" identity, poring over financial records, employee profiles, and company communications. It was a race against time, as The Syndicate's web of deception extended further than they could have ever imagined.

As they delved deeper into their investigation, they couldn't shake the feeling that they were being watched. Every move they made seemed to be anticipated, and their emails and phone calls felt like they were being monitored. The Syndicate was closing in, and the danger they faced was becoming increasingly palpable.

One evening, as Milan stepped out to meet a contact who claimed to have information about "X," he never returned. Panic rippled through the team as they realized that Milan had been abducted, presumably by The Syndicate.

With heavy hearts, they knew that they had reached a tipping point. The Syndicate was no longer content with shadowy manipulation; they were willing to resort to violence to protect their secrets. The intricate web of deception had tightened its grip, and the team was on the brink of a perilous confrontation with an adversary that seemed almost unbeatable.

The night stretched on, and the team sat in their dimly lit base, their determination unbroken but their hearts heavy with the knowledge that their pursuit of justice had pushed them to the edge. The Syndicate was no longer just a shadowy entity—it was a ruthless enemy that would stop at nothing to protect its secrets. In the dark corners of Prague, they were about to face their most formidable challenge yet, and the fate of WGC Holdings, the stock market, and perhaps even their own lives hung in the balance.

The Midnight Showdown

The air in Prague's historic district was thick with tension, and a sense of foreboding weighed heavily on Michael Stratton and his team. The abduction of Milan Novak, their reluctant ally from WGC Holdings, had sent shockwaves through their ranks. The Syndicate had shown that they were willing to use force to protect their secrets, and the team knew they were walking on a knife's edge.

As the clock struck midnight, a chilling silence descended over the city. The narrow streets of Prague, typically bustling with tourists and locals, now seemed eerily deserted. The team had gathered in their makeshift base, their laptops and evidence strewn across the table. They were determined to expose "X," the mole within WGC Holdings, and dismantle The Syndicate's network once and for all.

Emily, David, and Thomas worked tirelessly, tracing every lead and analyzing every piece of information they had gathered. Their investigation had led them to a shortlist of potential suspects within the company, but they needed concrete evidence to unmask "X."

Michael paced the room, his mind racing with thoughts of Milan's fate. The Syndicate had shown that they would stop at nothing to protect their secrets, and they had a mole within WGC Holdings who could compromise the team's efforts at any moment.

Just then, a dim light flickered to life outside their window, casting long shadows on the room's walls. Michael froze, his senses on high alert. The flickering light seemed deliberate, like a signal.

Emily turned to him, her eyes wide with realization. "It's a message, Michael. Someone's trying to communicate with us."

They rushed to the window and peered out into the dark alley below. There, illuminated by the faint glow of a lamppost, they saw a figure shrouded in shadows. It was Andrei, the contact from Bucharest who had led them to Petrov.

Andrei signaled for them to come down, his movements cautious. With trepidation, the team left their base and descended the narrow staircase, emerging into the moonlit alley.

"Andrei, what are you doing here?" Michael asked, his voice low.

Andrei's face was pale, his eyes filled with fear. "I heard about Milan's abduction. I had to find you. They're closing in on all of us."

The urgency in Andrei's voice was palpable. He explained that he had been in hiding since their encounter with The Syndicate in Bucharest, but he had managed to gather information about Milan's whereabouts. The Syndicate had taken him to a secluded villa in the Czech countryside, and time was running out.

"We can't let them harm Milan," Emily said, her voice resolute. "We have to rescue him."

Andrei nodded in agreement. "I can take you there, but you have to be prepared for anything. The Syndicate doesn't play by the rules."

The team knew the risks, but they had come too far to turn back now. With Andrei as their guide, they set out for the remote villa where Milan was being held captive. The journey took them through winding country roads, their car cutting through the darkness like a shadow.

As they approached the villa, a sense of unease settled over them. The isolated location, surrounded by dense woods, seemed like the perfect hideaway for The Syndicate. Andrei parked the car a discreet distance away, and they proceeded on foot, their footsteps silent on the gravel path.

The villa's imposing gates loomed ahead, guarded by two burly figures in dark suits. The team had to rely on stealth and strategy to get past them. With a distraction orchestrated by Andrei, they managed to slip through the gates and approach the villa undetected.

The night was still, and the villa's windows were shrouded in darkness. The team moved cautiously, their senses sharp, as they searched for any sign of Milan. It wasn't long before they heard muffled voices coming from a room on the ground floor.

With bated breath, they approached the room and peered through a crack in the door. Inside, they saw Milan, bound to a chair, his face bruised and bloodied. Standing over him was a menacing figure—the leader of The Syndicate's enforcers.

Emily's heart pounded as she realized that they were outnumbered and outgunned. They had walked straight into a trap. The Syndicate had anticipated their rescue attempt and had set a deadly ambush.

The enforcer turned toward the door, his eyes locking onto Michael and his team. In that moment, the room exploded into chaos. Gunfire echoed through the villa, and the team was forced to dive for cover.

Amidst the chaos, a fierce firefight erupted. Bullets whizzed through the air, shattering windows and sending shards of glass flying. Michael and his team fought valiantly, their determination unwavering, but the odds were stacked against them.

Andrei, who had joined the fray, provided much-needed support, but the enforcers were relentless. It was a battle of survival, and the team knew that failure meant not only their own demise but the loss of Milan as well.

As the firefight raged on, the room became a battleground of shadows and smoke, with the fate of Milan Novak hanging in the balance. The intricate web of deception had led them to this deadly showdown, and the outcome would determine the course of their relentless pursuit of justice.

The midnight showdown continued, a desperate struggle in the heart of darkness, as Michael Stratton and his team fought to rescue Milan and confront the ruthless enforcers of The Syndicate. The stakes had never been higher, and the line between victory and defeat was thinner than a razor's edge.

The Unmasking

The gunfire had subsided, leaving an eerie silence in the dimly lit room of the secluded villa. Smoke hung in the air, the acrid scent stinging their nostrils as Michael Stratton and his team emerged from their cover, their hearts pounding with adrenaline.

The room was in shambles, with shattered windows and bullet-riddled walls. The Syndicate's enforcers lay still on the floor, their menacing presence silenced forever. But there was no sign of Milan Novak.

Emily rushed to Milan's side, her heart sinking as she saw the state he was in. His face was swollen and bruised, blood seeping from a gash on his forehead. With trembling hands, she began to untie the ropes that bound him to the chair.

"Milan, can you hear me?" she whispered urgently, her voice filled with concern.

Milan's eyes fluttered open, and he winced in pain. "You came for me," he managed to say, his voice weak.

"We couldn't leave you behind," David replied, helping Emily free Milan from his restraints.

With Milan now liberated, the team turned their attention to the villa's other rooms, searching for any clues that might lead them to The Syndicate's true leaders. It was clear that this had been a mere outpost, a place to carry out their nefarious activities.

As they explored further, they discovered a hidden chamber beneath the villa—a secret lair that held a trove of documents, encrypted files, and surveillance equipment. It was a treasure trove of information that could expose the inner workings of The Syndicate.

With Emily's expertise, they began to decipher the encrypted files, uncovering a web of financial transactions, insider trading schemes, and a trail of corruption that reached into the highest echelons of power. The Syndicate's alliance with rogue traders like Viktor Petrov was laid bare, and it was clear that they had been manipulating the global markets for their own gain.

But the most shocking revelation came when they accessed a file marked "X." It contained detailed information about the mole within WGC Holdings—their identity, their role, and their connections. The team's relentless pursuit had finally paid off, and they now held the key to exposing The Syndicate's true leaders.

The mole was none other than a high-ranking executive within WGC Holdings—a person of immense influence named Evelyn Monroe. She had been colluding with The Syndicate for years, providing them with critical information and protecting their interests within the company.

"We have to expose Evelyn Monroe," Emily said, her voice determined. "She's the linchpin, the one who's been facilitating The Syndicate's operations from within."

Michael nodded in agreement. "But we have to be cautious. Evelyn is a powerful figure, and she'll do everything in her power to protect herself and

The Syndicate."

As they gathered the evidence, they knew that they had reached a critical juncture in their investigation. Exposing Evelyn Monroe and dismantling The Syndicate's network would be a dangerous undertaking, but it was a path they could not turn away from.

Their next move was clear—to confront Evelyn Monroe and bring her to justice. But it wouldn't be easy. The Syndicate had shown that they would stop at nothing to protect their secrets, and the team was now a formidable threat in their eyes.

With Milan by their side, still recovering from his ordeal but determined to make amends, they left the villa and returned to Prague. The city's ancient streets seemed to whisper their secrets, and the team knew that their journey was far from over.

The unmasking of Evelyn Monroe and The Syndicate's true leaders was the culmination of months of relentless pursuit. The intricate web of deception had unraveled, revealing a dangerous alliance that reached into the highest levels of power. As the team prepared to confront their adversaries, the stakes were higher than ever, and the fate of the financial world hung in the balance.

The Final Confrontation

The night had fallen over Prague like a heavy shroud as Michael Stratton and his team gathered in a dimly lit room to prepare for their final confrontation with Evelyn Monroe and The Syndicate. The evidence they had uncovered had exposed the intricate web of deception that had ensnared the financial world, and now, they were on the cusp of unmasking the true leaders behind the sinister alliance.

Their laptops glowed with incriminating documents, surveillance footage, and encrypted messages, all pointing to Evelyn Monroe's complicity in The Syndicate's operations. The team knew that confronting her would be perilous, but they had come too far to back down now.

Milan Novak, who had recovered significantly from his ordeal, sat among them, his determination burning brightly. He had become an integral part of their mission, determined to make amends for his unwitting role in The Syndicate's schemes.

"We have to be cautious," Michael cautioned, his voice low but resolute. "Evelyn Monroe is a powerful figure, and The Syndicate will defend her at all costs. We need a plan, a way to expose her without tipping our hand too soon."

Emily nodded in agreement. "We should gather as much evidence as possible to present to the authorities. The more concrete proof we have, the harder it will be for them to protect her."

With their plan in motion, the team set out to gather the final pieces of evidence needed to expose Evelyn Monroe's role in The Syndicate. It was a race against time, as they knew that once they made their move, The Syndicate would do everything in their power to silence them.

Days turned into weeks as they meticulously gathered the evidence they needed. They accessed confidential financial records, traced wire transfers, and compiled a comprehensive dossier that left no room for doubt. The Syndicate's nefarious activities were laid bare, and Evelyn Monroe's involvement was undeniable.

As they finalized their preparations, a sense of trepidation hung in the air. The Syndicate had shown that they were willing to resort to violence to protect their secrets, and the team knew that they were walking into a dangerous situation.

Finally, the day of reckoning arrived. The team had arranged a meeting with Evelyn Monroe at a discreet location—an abandoned warehouse on the outskirts of Prague. They had chosen the site carefully, ensuring that it was far removed from prying eyes.

The warehouse was dimly lit, its concrete walls covered in graffiti, and the air was thick with tension as they waited for Evelyn to arrive. Milan had arranged the meeting, using his connections to lure her into their trap.

Minutes turned into hours, and just as doubt began to creep in, the sound of approaching footsteps echoed through the empty space. The team tensed, their eyes fixed on the entrance.

Evelyn Monroe entered the warehouse, her expression composed but tinged with a hint of suspicion. She was a formidable figure, exuding an air of authority that matched her role within WGC Holdings.

"You wanted to meet?" Evelyn said, her voice cool and controlled.

Michael stepped forward, holding up the incriminating evidence they had gathered. "We know everything, Evelyn. Your role in The Syndicate's operations, your collusion with rogue traders, your manipulation of the global markets—it's all here."

Evelyn's mask of composure slipped for a fraction of a second, and then she regained her poise. "You have no proof of anything."

But Emily was already connecting her laptop to a projector, displaying the evidence on a blank wall. Financial records, surveillance footage, and encrypted messages flashed before them, leaving no room for denial.

"The evidence speaks for itself," Emily said, her voice steady. "We've traced every step of your involvement, and we have witnesses who can corroborate our claims."

Evelyn's face paled, and for a moment, it seemed as though she might attempt to flee. But she knew that there was no escape from the overwhelming weight of the evidence against her.

"You've cornered me," Evelyn admitted, her voice filled with resignation. "But you won't be able to stop The Syndicate. We have too many powerful allies."

Michael's resolve remained unshaken. "We'll take our chances. The world needs to know the truth about The Syndicate and those who protect them."

As the authorities were alerted to the evidence against Evelyn Monroe, her arrest became imminent. The Syndicate's intricate web of deception had unraveled, and the final confrontation had brought them to the brink of justice.

In the aftermath, as Evelyn was taken into custody, the team couldn't help but reflect on the harrowing journey they had undertaken. The Syndicate, once a formidable adversary, had been exposed, and its influence was on the wane.

The financial world, though scarred by their actions, could begin to heal, and the intricate web of deception that had ensnared it was finally coming apart. Michael Stratton and his team had confronted the darkness that lurked within the shadows, and in doing so, they had brought the relentless pursuit of justice to its culmination.

As they left the abandoned warehouse, the night air was filled with a sense of resolution. The intricate web of deception had been unmasked, and the team knew that their battle against corruption and collusion was far from over. But they had shown that even in the face of formidable adversaries, the relentless pursuit of justice could prevail.

The city of Prague, with its ancient streets and hidden secrets, bore witness to their final confrontation, a testament to the unwavering determination of those who were willing to expose the truth, no matter the cost.

www.ingramcontent.com/pod-product-compliance
Lightning Source LLC
LaVergne TN
LVHW061604070526
838199LV00077B/7171